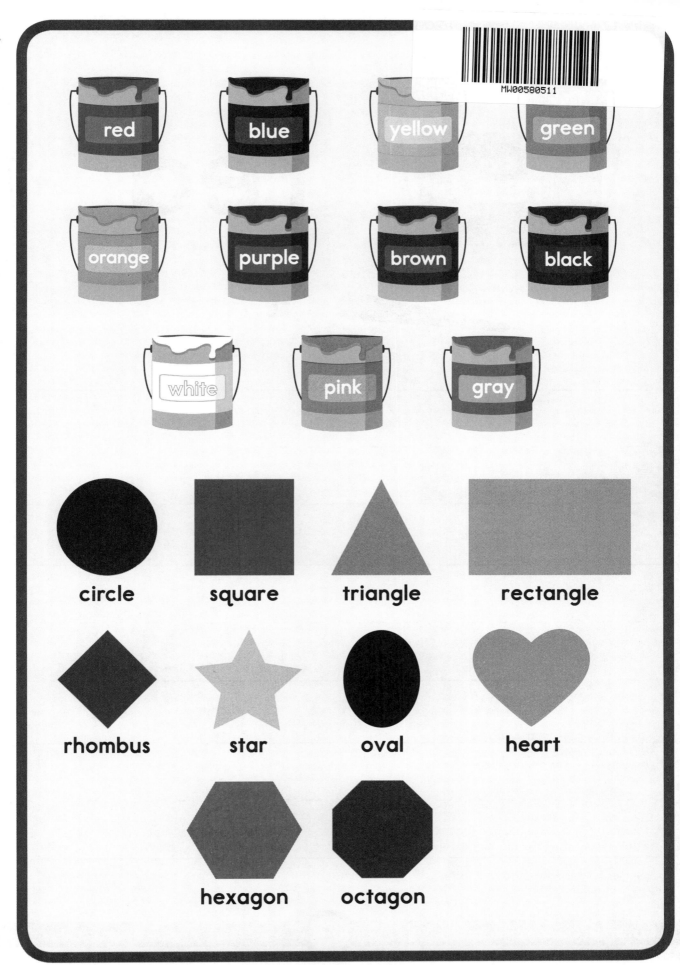

red
blue
yellow
green

orange
purple
brown
black

white
pink
gray

circle
square
triangle
rectangle

rhombus
star
oval
heart

hexagon
octagon

red

red

red

red

red

# Colors and Shapes

circle

purple

**purple**

purple purple

purple purple

Thinking Kids®
Carson-Dellosa Publishing LLC
Greensboro, North Carolina

Thinking Kids®
Carson-Dellosa Publishing LLC
PO Box 35665
Greensboro, NC 27425  USA

Printed in the USA • All rights reserved.
XX-XXXXXXXXX

ISBN  978-1-4838-4587-6

Color the apple

red.

Draw another object. Color it

red.

blue

blue blue

blue blue

Color the bird

blue.

Draw another object. Color it

blue.

yellow

yellow yellow

yellow yellow

Color the banana

yellow.

Draw another object. Color it

yellow.

red

red red red

blue

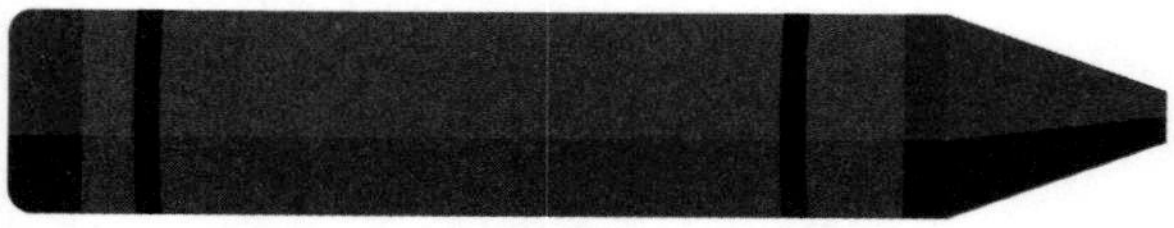

blue blue blue

yellow

yellow yellow

I see a

red

.

I see a

blue

.

I see a

yellow

.

green

green green

green green

Color the frog

green .

Draw another object. Color it

green .

orange

orange

orange

Color the pumpkin

orange.

Draw another object. Color it

orange.

# purple

purple purple

purple purple

# Color the grapes

purple.

# Draw another object. Color it

purple.

green

green     green

orange

orange orange

purple

purple purple

I see a

green

I see an

orange

I see a

purple

# brown

brown brown

brown brown

Color the horse

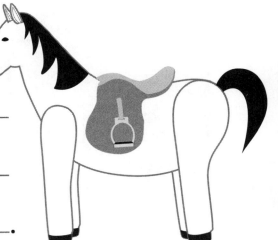

brown.

Draw another object. Color it

brown.

# black

black　black

black　black

Color the hat.

black.

Draw another object. Color it

black.

white

white white

white white

Color the lamb

white.

Draw another object. Color it

white.

brown

brown brown

black

black black

white

white white

I see a

brown

.

I see a

black

.

I see a

white

.

pink

pink     pink

pink     pink

Color the flower

pink.

Draw another object. Color it

pink.

# gray

gray gray

gray gray

Color the dolphin

gray.

Draw another object. Color it

gray.

pink

pink pink pink

gray

gray gray gray

## I can write my color words!

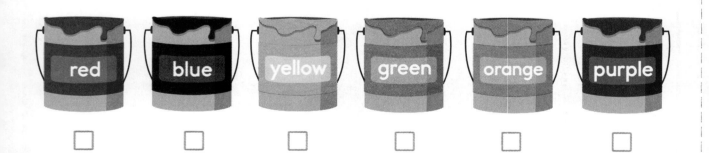

red    blue    yellow    green    orange    purple

☐    ☐    ☐    ☐    ☐    ☐

I see a

_____

------- pink -------

.

I see a

_____

------- gray -------

.

# circle

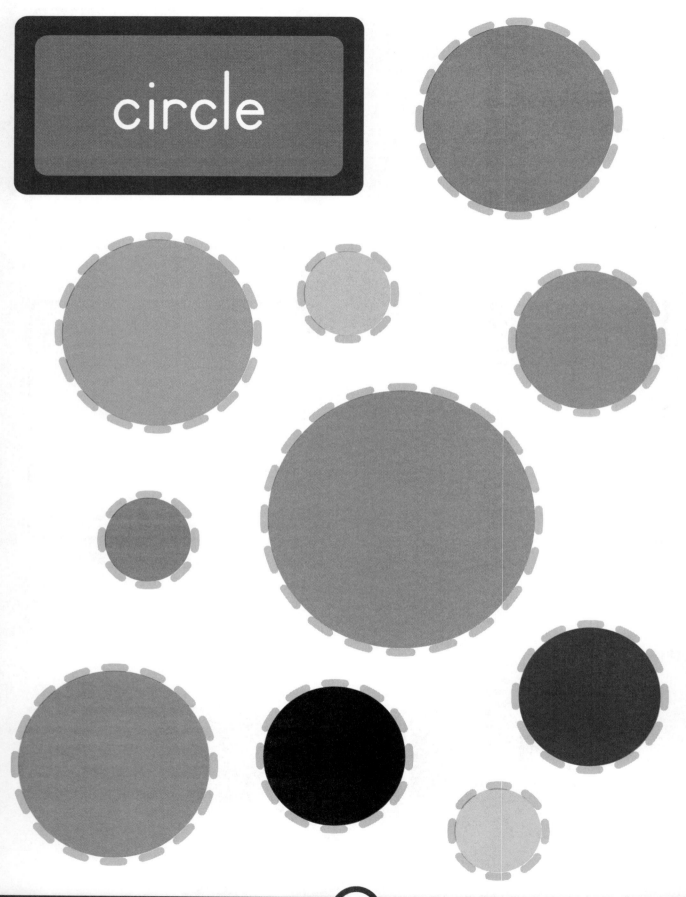

circle

circle circle

circle circle

The 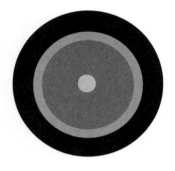 is shaped like

a circle .

The ⬤ is shaped like

a circle .

Draw an object shaped like

a circle .

# Trace the objects that are shaped like a circle.

YIELD

# square

square

square

square

The  is shaped like

a squ0re .

The  is shaped like

a square .

Draw an object shaped like

a square .

# Trace the objects that are shaped like a square.

# triangle

triangle

triangle

triangle

The  is shaped like

a triangle .

The  is shaped like

a triangle .

Draw an object shaped like

a triangle .

# Trace the objects that are shaped like a triangle.

# rectangle

rectangle

rectangle

rectangle

The  is shaped like

a rectangle.

The is shaped like

a rectangle.

Draw an object shaped like

a rectangle.

# Trace the objects that are shaped like a rectangle.

# rhombus

rhombus

rhombus

rhombus

The 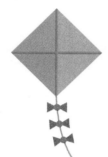 is shaped like

a rhombus .

The is shaped like

a rhombus .

Draw an object shaped like

a rhombus .

# Trace the objects that are shaped like a rhombus.

# oval

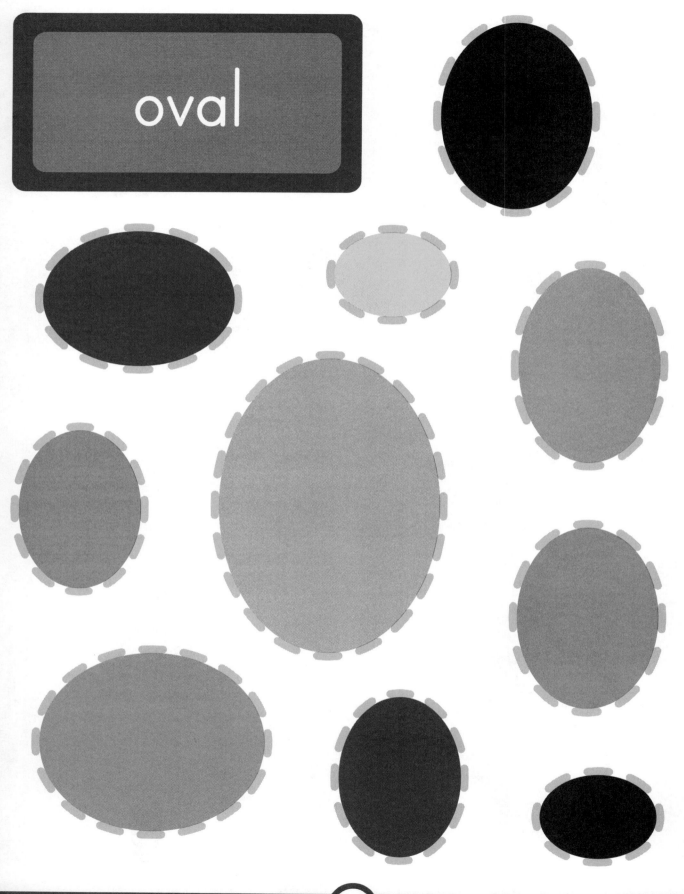

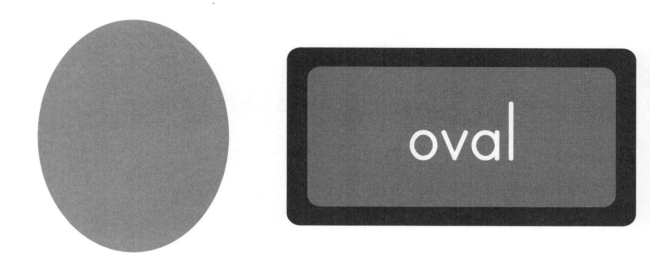

oval

oval     oval

oval     oval

The  is shaped like

an oval.

The  is shaped like

an oval.

Draw an object shaped like

an oval.

# Trace the objects that are shaped like an oval.

# star

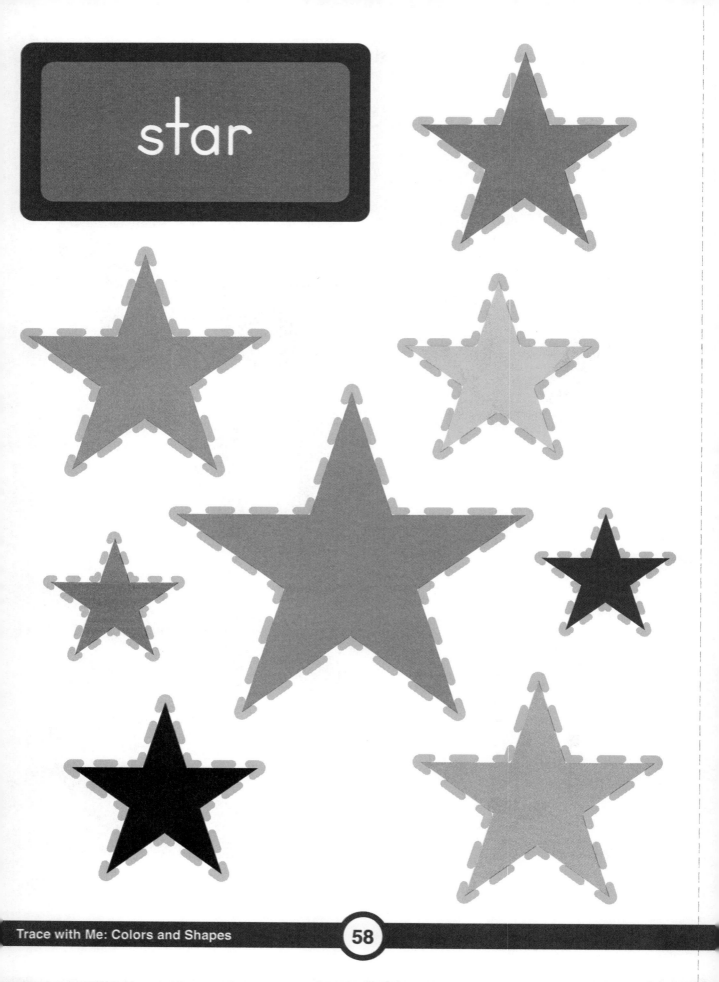

star

star        star

star        star

The 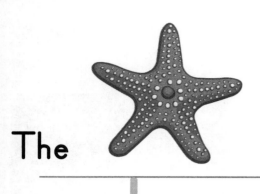 is shaped like

a star .

The  is shaped like

a star .

Draw an object shaped like

a star .

# Trace the objects that are shaped like a star.

# heart

heart

heart heart

heart heart

The           is shaped like

a heart.

The           is shaped like

a heart.

Draw an object shaped like

a heart.

# Trace the objects that are shaped like a heart.

# hexagon

hexagon

hexagon

hexagon

The 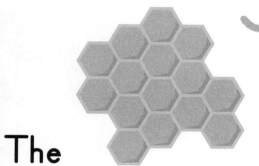 is shaped like

a hexagon.

The is shaped like

a hexagon.

Draw an object shaped like

a hexagon.

# Trace the objects that are shaped like a hexagon.

# octagon

octagon

octagon

octagon

The  is shaped like

an octagon.

The 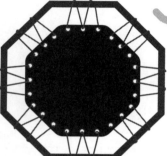 is shaped like

an octagon.

Draw an object shaped like

an octagon.

# Trace the objects that are shaped like an octagon.

# This is a

## circle.

# This is an

## oval.

**Trace the circles. Color them blue.**
**Trace the ovals. Color them red.**

# This is a

## square

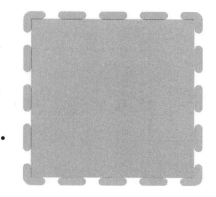

# This is a

## rectangle

**Trace the squares. Color them orange.**
**Trace the rectangles. Color them yellow.**

# This is a

## triangle.

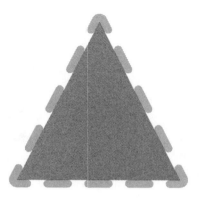

# This is a

## rhombus.

**Trace the triangles. Color them green.**
**Trace the rhombuses. Color them purple.**

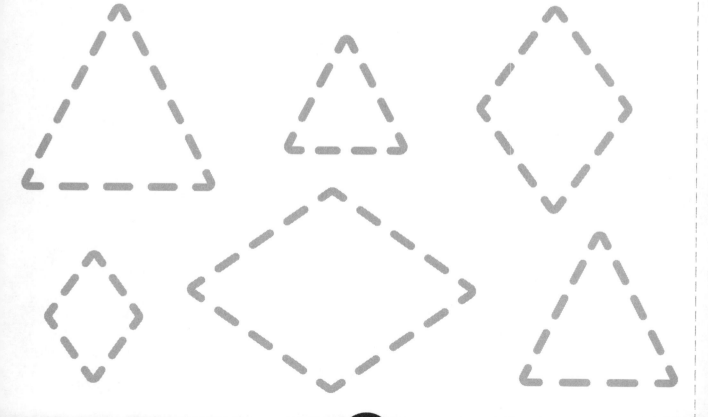

# This is a

## star

# This is a

## heart

Trace the stars. Color them yellow.
Trace the hearts. Color them red.

This is a

## hexagon .

This is an

## octagon .

**Trace the hexagons. Color them pink.**
**Trace the octagons. Color them brown.**

I can draw a _circle_.

I can draw a _square_.

I can draw a ___triangle___ .

I can draw a ___rectangle___ .

I can draw an _____oval_____.

I can draw a _____star_____.

I can draw a ___heart___.

I can draw a ___rhombus___.

I can draw a _____ hexagon _____.

I can draw an _____ octagon _____.

# Trace the circles.
# Color the circles red.

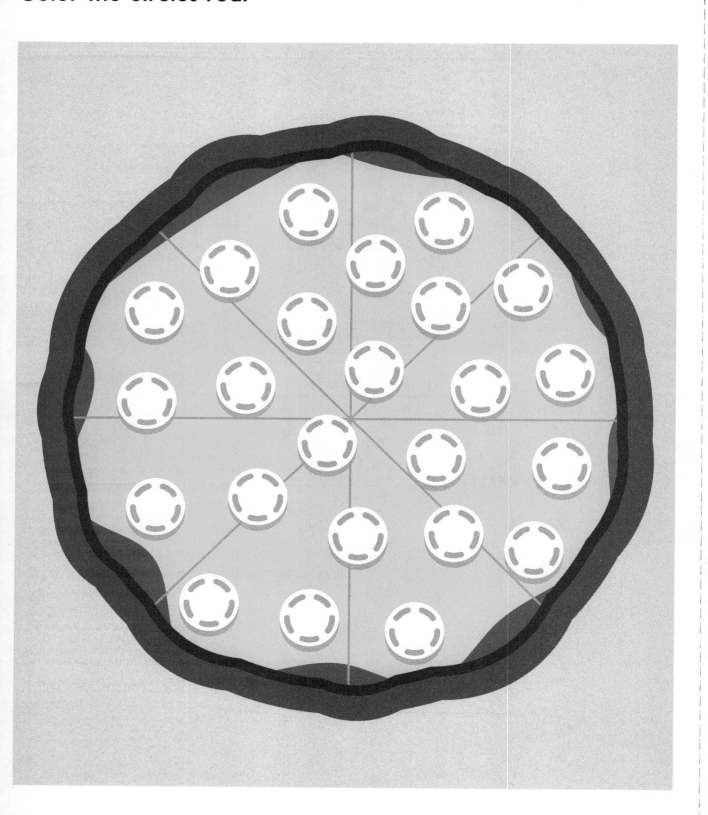

# Trace the circles.
# Color the circles purple.

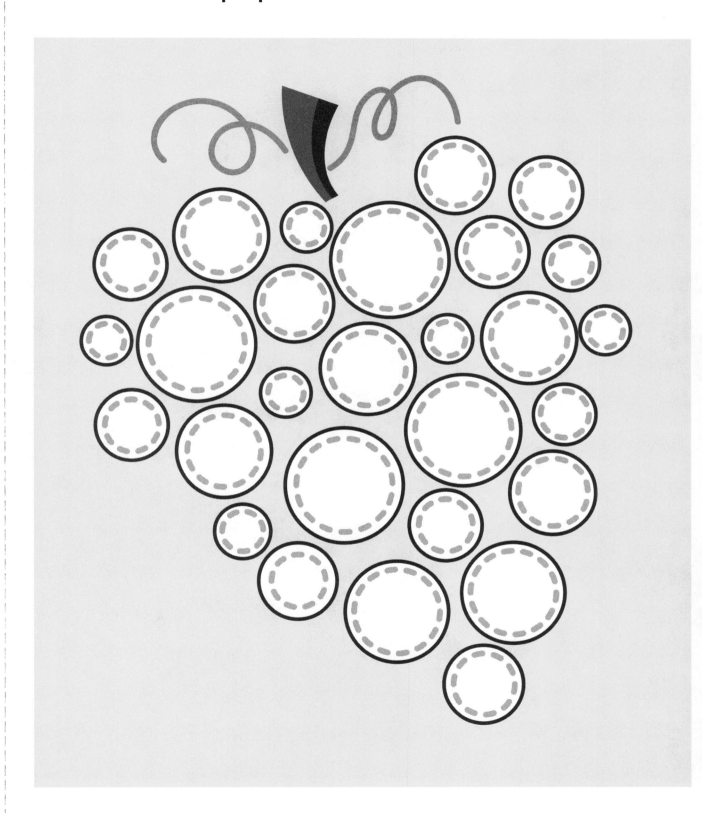

# Trace the circles.
# Color the circles brown.

# Trace the square.
# Color the square blue.

# Trace the squares.
# Color the squares green.

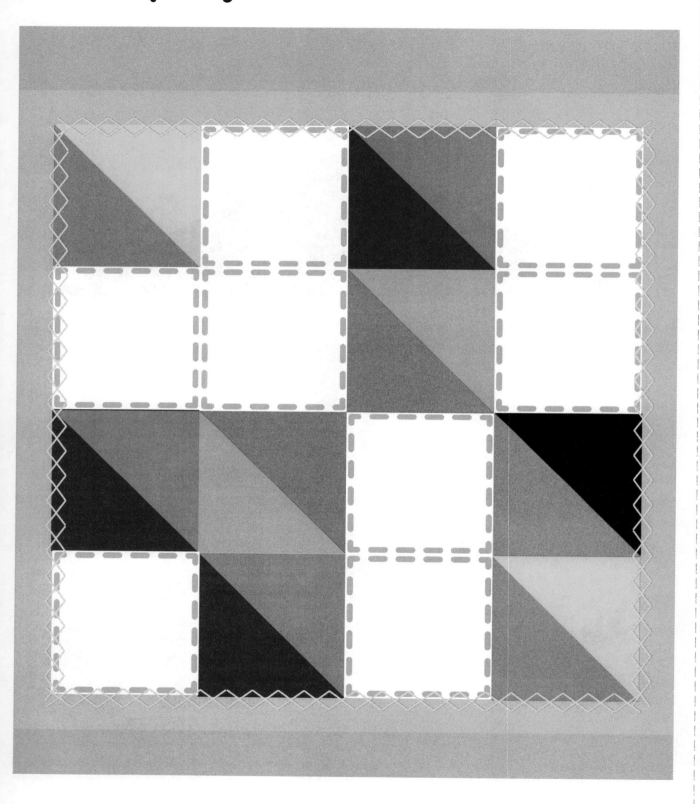

# Trace the squares.
# Color the squares purple.

# Trace the triangles.
## Color the triangles brown.

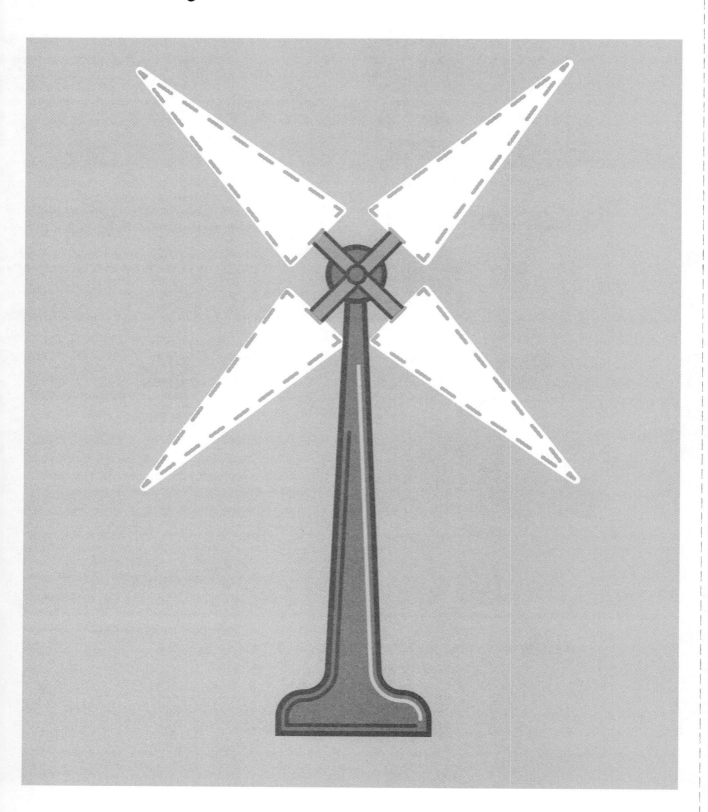

# Trace the triangles.
## Color the triangles blue.

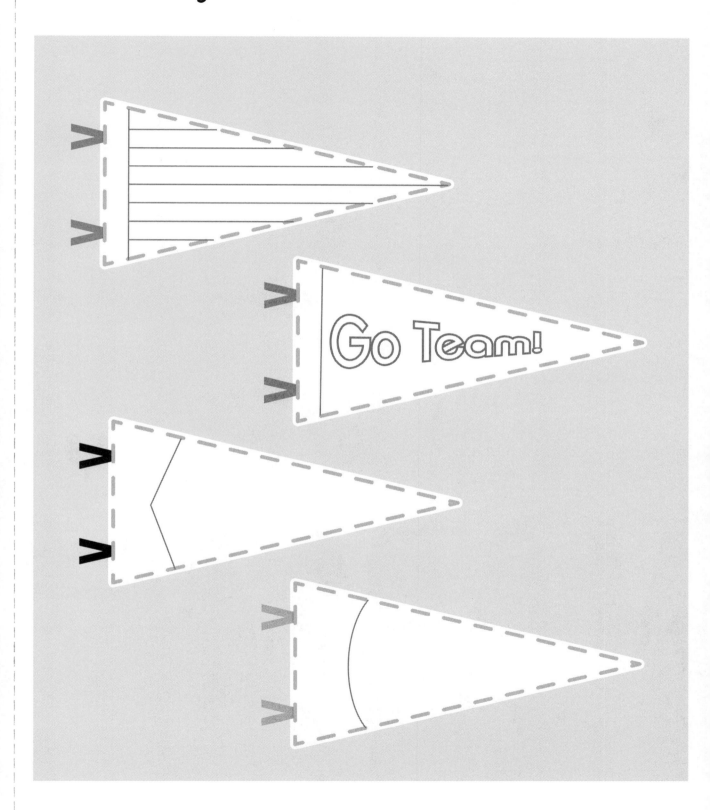

Go Team!

# Trace the triangles.
# Color the triangles orange.

# Trace the rectangles.
# Color the rectangles black.

# Trace the rectangles.
# Color the rectangles gray.

# Trace the rectangles.
# Color the rectangles orange.

# Trace the rhombuses.
# Color the rhombuses pink.

# Trace the rhombuses.
# Color the rhombuses orange.

# Trace the rhombus.
# Color the rhombus brown.

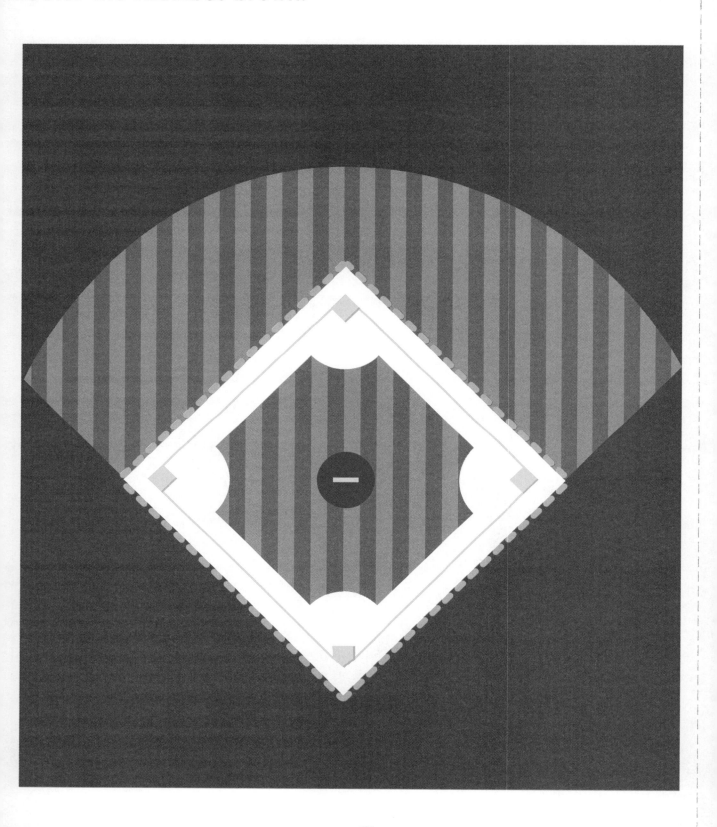

# Trace the stars.
# Color the stars yellow.

**Trace the star.**
**Color the star purple.**

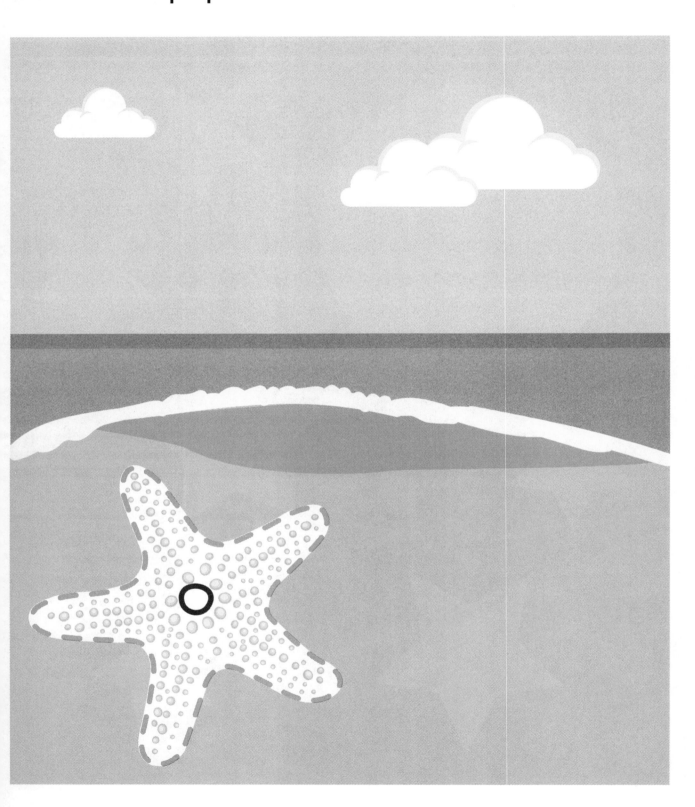

# Trace the ovals.
# Color the ovals green.

# Trace the ovals.
# Color the ovals blue.

welcome

# Trace the ovals.
# Color the ovals white.

# Trace the hearts.
# Color the hearts pink.

# Trace the hearts.
# Color the hearts red.

# Trace the hexagons.
# Color the hexagons yellow.

# Trace the hexagons.
# Color the hexagons gray.

# Trace the hexagons.
# Color the hexagons white.

# Trace the octagon.
# Color the octagon red.

# Trace the octagon.
# Color the octagon yellow.

# Trace the octagon.
# Color the octagon pink.

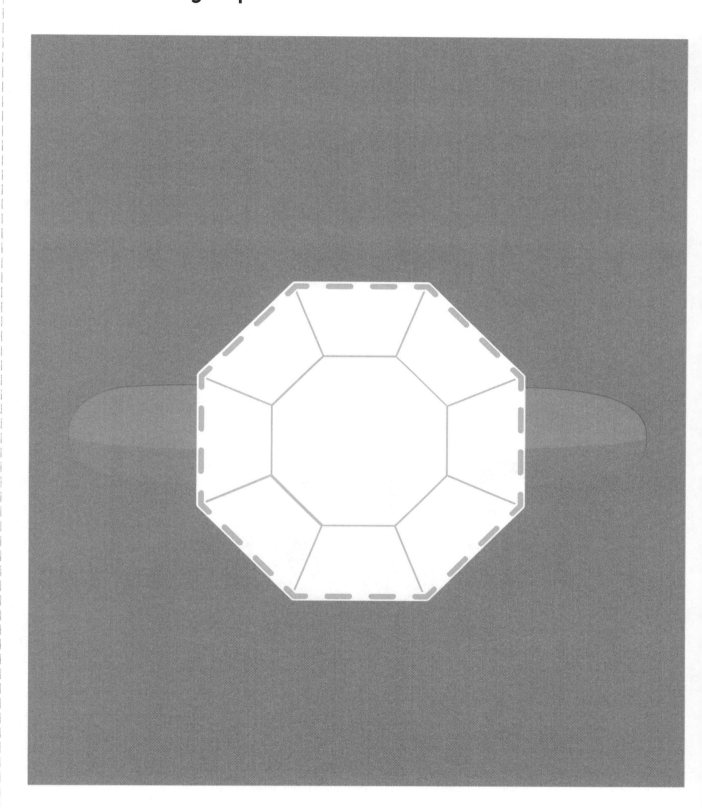

# Trace the shapes.
# Color the circles black.
# Color the squares blue.
# Color the octagon red.

# Trace the shapes.
Color the triangles brown.
Color the rectangles red.
Color the circles green.

Color the hearts pink.
Color the rhombus gray.

Trace the shapes.
Color the triangles green.
Color the stars yellow.
Color the square brown.

Color the rectangle black.
Color the circle white.

Trace the shapes.
Color the triangles blue.
Color the circle yellow.

Color the heart purple.
Color the oval red.

Trace the shapes.
Color the hexagons brown.
Color the oval yellow.
Color the rhombuses green.

Color the stars pink.
Color the hearts purple.

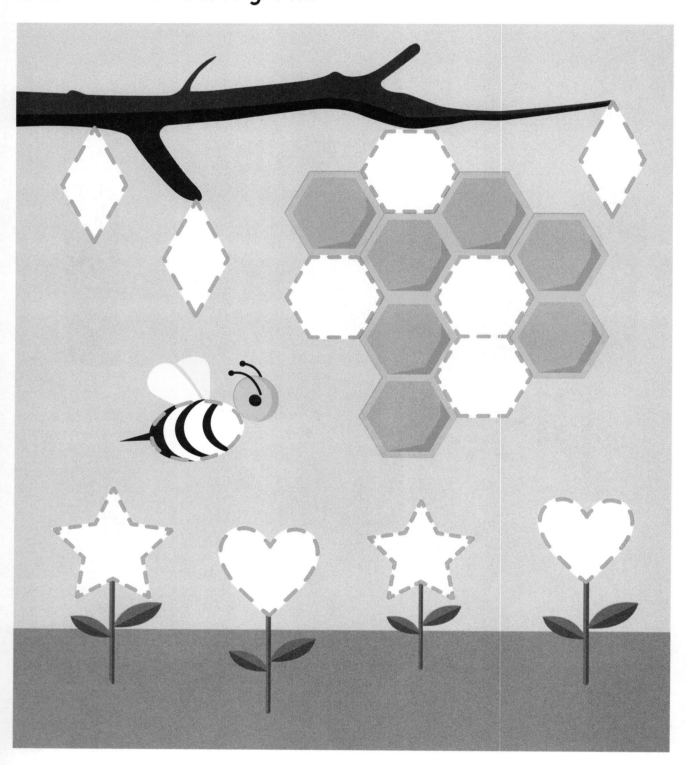

**Directions: Cut out the flash cards on pages 117-127. Review them with your child.**

Page is blank for cutting activity on previous page.

green

orange

purple

brown

Page is blank for cutting activity on previous page.

**black**

**white**

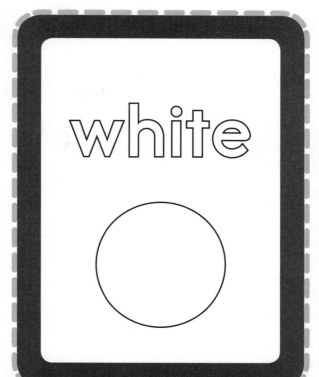

**pink**

**gray**

Page is blank for cutting activity on previous page.

# circle

# square

# triangle

# rectangle

Page is blank for cutting activity on previous page.

**rhombus**

**star**

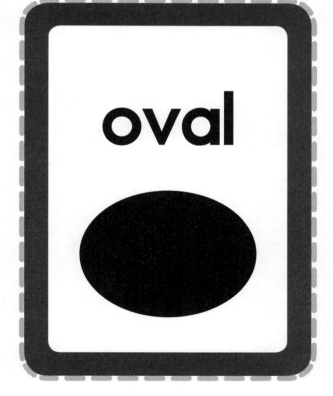

**oval**

**heart**

Page is blank for cutting activity on previous page.

# hexagon

# octagon

Page is blank for cutting activity on previous page.